GRAND SLAM

•A COLLECTION OF POEMS•

ALAN KLEIMAN

COPYRIGHT © 2013 BY ALAN S. KLEIMAN

All rights reserved
All pickles preserved
No song too long
No river too wide
Won't you be my bride
(said the lion to the pride)
Inside.

Front cover illustration © 2012 by John Newsom
Cover and book design by Lisa Hollander

ISBN-13: 978-0615857718
ISBN-10: 061585771X

Available from Crisis Chronicles Press
3344 West 105th Street #4
press.crisischronicles.com
www.Amazon.com

TABLE OF CONTENTS

Dedication	1
Puppy Love	2
Creativity at its Best	3
Herring Day	4
Centerfold	6
Sardines	8
Bad Theft	9
Joe Paloo	10
More	11
Tomorrow	12
What Tales	16
Spring	17
I Don't Wish Bluebirds	18
Meat on the Grill	20
Barn Reflected	21
Marshland Views	22
No Subjects	23
Dancing with Varèse	24
Changing Skies	25
Slow Dancing	26
Startling	29
Feta Dip	30
I Have No Plume	32
Wanting Girls	33
Sliver Removers and Pizzaholics	34
Sturgeon Moon	36

ACKNOWLEDGEMENTS:

Thank you to the editors of the journals where these poems first appeared:

Bad Theft – The Bicycle Review
Centerfold – Camel Saloon
Changing Skies – Vox Poetica
Dancing with Varèse – Blue Fifth Review
No Subjects – Pyrta
More – Right Hand Pointing
Puppy Love – Eskimo Pie
Slow Dancing – The Criterion
Spring – Lyrical Lip Service
Startling – Montucky Review
What Tales – Words Dance

DEDICATION

Roses are red hot
Posies are not hot
Tomatoes taste great
I dedicate this poem
To home plate.

PUPPY LOVE

Oh baby, puppy love,
It's like springtime
For rednecks
Springtime
In the midst of the monsoon
Springtime when all cicadas
Are screaming their legs off
At full bore
And there's a lightning storm
And thunder
And Jeter just hit a GRAND SLAM home run
In the bottom of the 9th 2 outs 2 strikes
And the Yankees win the WORLD SERIES

And there's some passion
And mooning and spooning
And holding hands
And that kind of mushy stuff too
But that's mostly for girls
Cause for guys they're thinking
Home Run Derby firecrackers
And red hot tamales.

CREATIVITY AT ITS BEST

To be or not to be
That is the answer to our prayers
I made up the first line
I'm proud of it
It's catchy
Like Beethoven's Fifth
I made that up too
This morning
I am having a burst of creativity
Let it flow let it flow let it flow.

HERRING DAY

Yesterday the noise was deafening
for its utter lack thereof
"Nothing doing ma'am" he said
to the woman in the orange hair
Can you imagine? Orange hair
at a party like this?
Well we just picked up our tool chest
and headed briskly out the door
not even stopping along the way
for fresh fish
or cucumber salad
nestling in glass bowls
painted on each side
with the letters "RJG"
and the numbers "88"
in blue ink below.
"That's weird" he was heard to mumble
and swiftly he climbed the stairs
dreaming not so much of
ice cream but of the song
the ice cream vendor sang
at the end of the day
when it was time to
wash the scoops
and put away the cones.

'Mary had a little lamb'
sounded something
like the main theme
but I tell you
that theme was far more minor
in parts and near atonal in others
so why that association
was even raised
is a red herring
which brings us back to the reason
for this tale at all.
Today is Herring Day in fine NY City.

> "The eagerly anticipated arrival of 'nieuwe maatjes' herring from Holland, the tasty delicacy from the waters of the Netherlands, occurs on Tuesday afternoon, June 7, at the historic Grand Central Oyster Bar. The year-long wait is almost over. Opening ceremonies include the 'Official First Tasting' of Dutch Herring this year."
> – THE WAITING HAS BEEN ROUGH.

CENTERFOLD

But I'm usually more shy
I don't centerfold regularly
I don't centerfold happily
I centerfolded only a time or two my whole life
And I wasn't thrilled centerfolding at all.

Shyness doesn't mean you are shy
It doesn't mean you want to die
Or hide from each face
like a butterfly.

It doesn't mean you are timid
Looking
or speak with a quiet sound
or laugh only when laughed at
or sing when the voice is laryngitis hoarse
when even a cry won't sound.

Shy's when inside you're scared
and say truth to yourself
Never
When you must be shy
because pain bars the doors.

Even a fire in the stables
won't let the horse escape.
Burn before leaving
Put water in a dish left outside the stall
and think it will hold back the flames.

Only water will lash the storms
of rage, the visions of self
crashing the rocky shore
Hard.

The dish won't burn,
like the burning bush. Truth
won't escape. Flames
won't lick the dew off grass or upper lip.

Stand tall
Remember
Duty has no meaning in a colored light
Shifting sands mean everything.

SARDINES

Thursday morning before noon
when candles from the night
still cracked cold
sitting in ice melt and cigarette butts.

I sat at a table
with a crayon for pencil
wondering morning thoughts
But breakfast thoughts?
or lunch thoughts?

I wanted sardines
and Coke instead of beer.

Clouds edged the world
the sun spit in wisps
too small to warm the insides
but bright enough to
put shades on my eyes for shelter.

It wasn't brunch or lunch
I wanted
but night itself
if you looked far enough.

BAD THEFT

My bike was stolen tonight
My steady ride forever
Taken
With just a cut lock in its place
A business card for the crook
The bum who took it away.

JOE PALOO

"Jooooooeee," "Joooeeeeeeeey"

"Joe Pallooooooooooo"
"Joe"

Soft wispy Mississipp swamp drawl

"Palloooooooooo"

Hazelmist swamp rat

"Joe, where"

Hollow, dragnet sounds in marble night

"are yoouuuuu?" "ooooooooooo"
"Where arrrrrrre..."
"I love you Joeeeee"
"I love you Joooeeeeeey"

Slow.
Cloud.
Wet.
Mist. Dark. Alabam southern.

"Joe Palloo, Joe Palloo
Joe Palloo"

MORE

Kiss me a hundred times
and then a thousand
and then more than that
and then even more
and you will begin
to touch
the spot where
I want to kiss you more.

TOMORROW

Tomorrow never comes
but it's here right now
in the living room with me
right next to my chair
the grayish one with the stripes
from the old days in the office
when sitting in the corner
in the cushy chair
was like taking a holiday
in Spain or Paris
even before the airlines needed
to whisk you away
to St. Tropez.

I had a trophy there
an award performance
remembered fondly by the walls,
the sheet rock
even the window
the fluorescent lights
that watched
from their off position
the whole dance
played out against gray carpet
a few chairs
and a table or two.

Well there it was in this setting
where those miraculous 40's passed by
where the power of our life
was realized
where the strength of mature adulthood
took its mark and left it
in strength
as powerful as
we were going to be

That's where we made our mark
That's where we became
from our 30's
Boy wonders on the move
to our 40's
boy wonders having moved life,
art, music, sex, divorce, children,
partnerships, new cars, new homes,
all these things took shape in the 40's
so rich, so strident, so full
of taste buds' delight,
yet filled with the lack of self awareness
that only hindsight brings to bear.

Here the 50's redound
what do they speak of
but futures with a different sense of self

Futures with a less powerful push
with less oomph than "I can do it"
Oh, I can do it Oh yes,
but sometimes in the mirror
of my shadow on the walk
or just watching the flip
of a leg over a bike
I see the movement
of an old man
the stiffness that places
the fluid movements of youth
into old man categories
and straightens the curves
and makes the leg less swoopier
It's a hint but it's there

We have all seen old men
and old women dance
It's that dance that wants to audition now
for the new part that smiles
that says Polident instead of Crest
We see it as not bad or sad –
But changed so much
that even Autumn
can be tolerated now
even Autumn
that hurt me so in the past
that made me cry with its meanness
its stealing of the warmth
of the long days,
of the chirping nights,

That mean harsh Autumn
all dressed up in fancy clothes
never fooled me
I hated its mean endings
and its gifts
of ice cold gray streets
That Autumn, that same Autumn
comes now like an old non-friend
Almost tolerable
sometimes showing
its good side
its sweetness smirking
behind its flash
and I can say, Ha –
Here's old Autumn again –
He'll be gone before the night is up
Let's see his dress and his swank this year
because Spring, our beloved,
will be here before you can say blink.

Because with age comes speed
comes life as a roller blade wheel
that spins and circles
at its own momentum
with no rhyme or reason
and that's how it is today
Some say hooray?

WHAT TALES

The old barn captured
in a sunny day-light print
the years of stories
mere hints.

The tires in the loft
four summers, one snow,
the spare?

Folks must have left in winter
snow treads still mounted,
heading north out of town.
The summer treads could stay
like bathing suits in January.

Hey, were those wheels
from that broken down Pontiac,
sold "as is"
tires forgotten?

If hay could speak,
what tales, what tales...

Walls lined like wrinkled brows
keeping silent,
what tales.

Out in the field
her small feet earthbound
she stood and looked around
in every direction
searching.

SPRING

I never saw a spring I didn't like.
There've been cold ones
Wet ones,
And cloudy glum ones
But I loved them all.

One time
After crocuses said hello
And daffodils waved,
Snow came
As if to say
Stop having fun.

But we couldn't.
Sun angles broaden
Dusks arrive later
Birds and worms
Make rackets
Poking their noses at will.

Mud perfume fills our lungs
Breaths deepen and slow
Postures brighten
Life engages once more
And, sweet as honey,
We awaken too.

I DON'T WISH BLUEBIRDS

I had a surprise call today
But really what call
Is not a surprise
Surprise at the ordinary "Hi"
Or surprise from Joe from school
Or from a cousin not seen
Since Jimmy Carter
Or a love
Unrequited forever.
Over and over suits ring us up
To talk about the day
Or hour
When Shylock asks
For the impossible pound.

Never will I give life
To succor
But I will hold the babe in my arms
And the child in the soul
From as deep within
As I can find
Glory Hallelujah.

I hope I'll discover where men toil
And people change
From regular to someone
To mattering to care
And be cared about

I don't look to find a soul
But I look for the soul
To find me
In my woods adrift
In my ship sputtering
Where nothing has to give direction
Where nothing has to cry the vector
Where only albatrosses circling near
Dry in the throat
Pull us to the light.

I don't wish bluebirds
Or pomegranate roots
But still I wish grapes
And bunches
Of delicate fingers
Blond hair green eyes
Smiles inside and love
Love like a cat
Like a bird
Like a fish
Like a song
Reverberating the night
Till we dress
Descend despair
And delouse our cigarettes,
Free to endure
Till death do us part.

MEAT ON THE GRILL

Fat well cut
the loon is a goon
don't despair
when you're not there

Loon tunes
will run through your ear
you try to recall exactly
but you recall 98%

Sad you missed the last note
be thankful you heard it rare.

You're not afraid
for someone
with meat on the grill.

BARN REFLECTED

It's as beautiful
as made up.

I never saw it before
Doubled in water.

How'd you catch it
he thought
How'd you get
so lucky
to have the eye
and the
camera
in the same place
and time
in your head
and hand.

MARSHLAND VIEWS

Memories of dawns long past
Songs of dusks recently past
Birds flying by over marshland views
Scattered with herons and a crab or two

Too much to dream of
Too much to consider
Too much to sing about
Time to have dinner

Closing of the sky to thoughts and games
Retire says the judge to the game warden again
Retire says the officer to the vegetable keeper cop

Time passes, take a stroll
And try the new pizza
Treat your mouth to some fancy
And call in the morning
Of the new day

NO SUBJECTS

I wrote lots more poems
but there were no subjects
available today.

So I returned the words to their
spaces in the dictionary
and put the letters back in the
alphabet
until
suitable subjects arise.

Then I need to just whistle
and the words
come together
as before.

DANCING WITH VARÈSE

I'm having a total Varèse night of it
Sad your peels are closed
But happy to know
We are in the same alphabet
And always inundated with sweetness
At the sound of your footsteps
In the opening paragraph.

Not content at slithering
I relish hot dogs, mustard and petards
Where men are men
And girls go to the bathroom giggling
Hoping for friendship
When it may be just noise
Or not
Because society craves invention
Progress peaks at postal hours
And men who carry doors with them
At every turn open them
Extend an arm and say
Slap me five Cucamonga
I just married your brother.

Tales like that and alphabet soup
Occur strangely in peach filled bowls
Except when the cream is loose and
You can taste it on your lips
Like tonight I hope I pray I fear
Kiss the cat Margaret.

CHANGING SKIES

I like spitting out
bruised chewed and swallowed sky
wonder what's behind
that spit that eye

the rabbit hair and samovar
eclectic wanderings
across boundaries
push identities to new shades

contact lenses give way
to glasses,
and roses
give way to sky views

perhaps where even bats
get the boot.

SLOW DANCING

Thirty-three days ago
Bartholome's son
Knocked on my door asking
Help me for I have sinned.

Don't ask directions
Ask what love is about
Don't ask for songs
Ask what words are about
Don't cry me a river
Row to Europe
Find Emily
And call the earth good morning.

Then one day
After people heard
About tombstones
They left the shack
Ate pasta in the streets
And said
There's no bones but an old dog's.

Don't resurrect
Josephus in my living room
We have no space
For the past

Put the future someplace else
Redact the letters that make words
Too intelligible
Masses have rights to read
To sing to dance to bowl
Every alley is open
To Jurassic members of our club
Won't you pay your dues
And push open the door
To the new world
Where sayonara means hello
And where sukiyaki means
How do you like my neighbor's wife's legs?

The jackets we wear
With our name
In the lining
Anchor too deeply.
Why "out of sight out of mind"
Allows existence
Is a puzzle for the ages
Dumb lucky
We find parallel hotel rooms
With fantasy so real
The border shifts
To Ha! I am alive again.

Call me Jack for today
And John tomorrow
Edith the next
And Mary Joe on Friday.
Perhaps I will retire now
Into the boudoir
Who will I find there
To dine with
Sophie from the office?
Gertrude from the bookstore?
Or Melissa alive in the book of names?

Tomorrow I have no intention
Of stopping anywhere.
Not to be besotted
For your pleasure
And the experience of loving
Loving what passes as sop
Soup is nicer to say
The Emperor's clothes
Don't fit anymore.

STARTLING

The poet arrived last night
In New York City
At the University
Amidst great fanfare.

She introduced a poem
Recalling how
In a small museum
Upon first sight
Of a 6 inch Daphne sculpture

Her breathing had changed.

After that startling revelation
All the rest was just words.

FETA DIP

I dipped I saw
I conquered
I was conquered

red pesto in the air
swirled in smoke whiffs
above my hair

there was little left to say
little left unsaid

swirling white dip
creased
with pretzel grooves
your favorite

what is feta
among Amerkins

good
but never home
great
but not home-cooked
fill-the-hole
food
know where you live
food

cocktail franks and colored toothpicks

gimme shelter
helter skelter
something I can
hang my
hat on
and let a tear flow if
that's life

in Amarakin Amtrak
outback.

I HAVE NO PLUME

I have no answer
for exhaling
no plume
to call Valerie
I only see Bridgeport factories
and sad liberations
of nothingness
ridiculed by the sun.

The rain came
without water yesterday.
What were we to do?

Because the time to answer
had expired
and we had our mouths closed
like a drum skin
at dawn.

WANTING GIRLS

My mother wanted only girls but got seven boys
three white ones
a black
and some other kinds.

Fourteen years she worked to put her boys
through finishing school,
but they never finished.
They were odd and crude
preferring to spit on pretty women
rather than say hello
or take a dance.
They'd cop a feel
in the elevators
and even on busses.

Why, I was just seven years old
when she came up to me and said,
How about a lay?
Not with my wife you don't,
said the chicken (crossing the road).

SLIVER REMOVERS AND PIZZAHOLICS

I'm not bad or green today
I'm sort of ordinary
Sitting at my desk
Wearing a tie.
It's in front of my shirt.

I have a cup of pencils
Clips, pens,
Screen with its limited menu
No games, no girls,
No socializing,
Work.

On my left an inbox
With more papers,
An empty couch
A painting by a man just dead,
A plant I've ceased caring for
Perhaps like a wanton son
Who will return
Perhaps while there is still life.

"I can understand how one can be confused"
Someone in the hall says.
Perplexing statement, I think,
For midday.

"Make it happen"
Can be a plan
So can "Eat rhubarb"

"Call a plumber"
or "Get your teeth cleaned."

Allusions to actions and
Place holders
For do-nothing
Days.

"Write a poem"
Can ice the cake
And put dreams
Below the pillow.

I'll need cleaning-lady day soon
He thought,
To wash the sink of socks
And the chairs of pedantry.
"I brushed my teeth" he yelled
Now let me close the tube tight

So toothpaste breath perfume
Does not become
The new name of the house
Amongst honkeys,
Sliver removers
And pizzaholics.

Tomorrow is just too
Late for the dance.

STURGEON MOON

So hard the sky
The rain pelting, stinging
No one recalled harsher blasts.

Dylan songs, the new stuff,
Lit the radio
But you couldn't hear the music.

He wanted to dance
To fill in
The unheard gaps
But she refused
Her rubber boots by the hall,

The August full moon
Compelling him,
Hidden though it was,
Behind the clouds.

www.ingramcontent.com/pod-product-compliance
Lightning Source LLC
Chambersburg PA
CBHW041527090426
42736CB00035B/36